STRUCTURAL WONDERS
# GIZA PYRAMIDS

opp

FOCUS
READERS
NAVIGATOR

# WWW.FOCUSREADERS.COM

Focus Readers is distributed by North Star Editions:
sales@northstareditions.com | 888-417-0195

Produced for Focus Readers by Red Line Editorial.

Photographs ©: Shutterstock Images, cover, 1, 4–5, 7, 9, 10–11, 29; Science History Images/ Alamy, 13; Henning Dalhoff/Science Source, 15; Christian Jegou/Science Source, 16–17; Mikkel Juul Jensen/Science Source, 19; Ministry of Antiquities/AP Images, 21; Nariman El-Mofty/AP Images, 23, 27; iStockphoto, 24–25

**Library of Congress Cataloging-in-Publication Data**
Names: Jopp, Kelsey, 1993- author.
Title: Giza pyramids / by Kelsey Jopp.
Description: Lake Elmo, MN : Focus Readers, [2023] | Series: Structural
  wonders | Includes bibliographical references (page 32) and index. |
  Audience: Grades 4-6
Identifiers: LCCN 2022026203 (print) | LCCN 2022026204 (ebook) | ISBN
  9781637394793 (hardcover) | ISBN 9781637395165 (paperback) | ISBN
  9781637395851 (pdf) | ISBN 9781637395530 (ebook)
Subjects: LCSH: Pyramids--Egypt--Jīzah--Juvenile literature. | Jīzah
  (Egypt)--Antiquities--Juvenile literature.
Classification: LCC DT63 .J66 2023  (print) | LCC DT63  (ebook) | DDC
  932/.2--dc23/eng/20220615
LC record available at https://lccn.loc.gov/2022026203
LC ebook record available at https://lccn.loc.gov/2022026204

Printed in the United States of America
Mankato, MN
012023

# ABOUT THE AUTHOR

Kelsey Jopp is an editor, writer, and lifelong learner. She lives in Minnesota, where she enjoys swimming in lakes and playing endless fetch with her sheltie, Teddy.

# TABLE OF CONTENTS

# CHAPTER 1

# A WORLD WONDER

Gusts of hot wind blow sand across the desert. Noises from the nearby city float in the air. Looming tall above the land are the Giza Pyramids. They glow orange-brown in the sun. The pyramids are thousands of years old. Yet still they stand. People travel from around the world to see them.

**Some people ride camels when they visit the Giza Pyramids.**

The Giza Pyramids are in northern Egypt. They sit on the Giza Plateau. This is a raised area of flat, rocky land. Next to the pyramids is the busy city of Giza. The Nile River is also nearby. It is one of the longest rivers in the world. Across the river is Cairo, Egypt's capital city.

Several pyramids make up the Giza site. A pyramid is a structure with triangle-shaped sides. The sides meet in a point at the top. Most pyramids have four sides and a square base. They are built from large, stacked stones.

At Giza, there are three large pyramids. The largest is the Great Pyramid. This structure was built for King Khufu in

The modern city of Giza extends to the edge of the pyramid site.

approximately 2550 BCE. Khufu's son, King Khafre, had the second pyramid built. The third pyramid was built for King Menkaure.

Each of the three large pyramids has a **complex**. Each complex includes smaller pyramids. These are called queen pyramids. There are also temples, cemeteries, and other features. One example is the Great Sphinx. This large statue features a lion's body and a king's head.

The Great Pyramid is one of the Seven Wonders of the Ancient World. These were famous structures in the Middle East and Europe. The Great Pyramid is the only one still standing. It is also the oldest. The Great Pyramid is 450 feet (137 m) tall. For more than 3,000 years, it was the tallest building in the world.

This pyramid is made of 2.3 million blocks of stone. It weighs 5.75 million tons (5.22 million metric tons). The huge structure amazed ancient Egyptians. It continues to amaze people today.

# GIZA PYRAMID COMPLEX

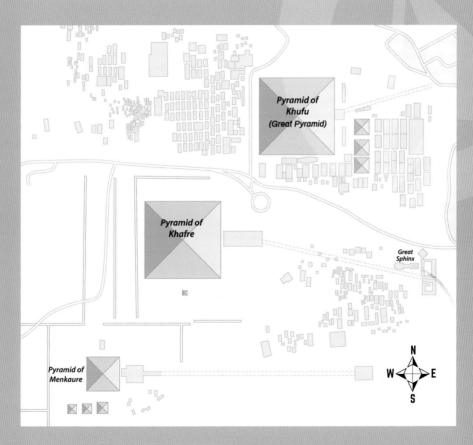

Pyramid of Khufu (Great Pyramid)

Pyramid of Khafre

Great Sphinx

Pyramid of Menkaure

# CHAPTER 2

# THE MYSTERY OF GIZA

The Giza Pyramids were built to be tombs for Egypt's **pharaohs**. A tomb holds the body of a person who has died. Many people in ancient Egypt were buried in tombs. But most tombs were small. They were not as grand as the pyramids.

The Giza Pyramids are mostly solid. However, there are small **chambers**

**Each stone block weighs approximately 5,000 pounds (2,300 kg).**

inside. The Great Pyramid has the King's Chamber and the Queen's Chamber. It also has a tall hallway called the Grand Gallery.

Tunnels at the base of each pyramid lead to underground chambers. King Menkaure and King Khafre were buried in these chambers. But the underground area of the Great Pyramid was not finished. King Khufu was buried inside the King's Chamber instead.

The Old Kingdom of Egypt is known as the Pyramid Age. This period lasted from approximately 2600 to 2200 BCE. During this time, more than 100 pyramids were built. The first pyramids were

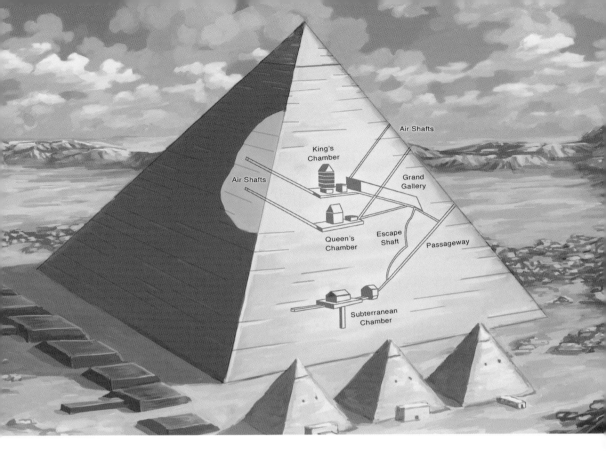

This illustration shows the chambers inside the Great Pyramid.

step pyramids. The sides of the pyramids looked like stairs. Later on, the Egyptians built true pyramids. These pyramids had smooth sides.

No one knows how the pyramids were built. Ancient Egyptians did not have today's technology. Some historians believe the Egyptians used wooden ramps. They think builders used the ramps to carry up the stones. As the pyramids were made taller, so were the ramps. Other historians say this idea is wrong. They think Egypt did not have enough wood to build so many ramps.

## CHANGING COLOR

The pyramids were not always brown. In ancient times, the Great Pyramid was white. It had an outer layer of white limestone. These stones were moved from across the Nile River. The white limestone made the pyramid shine in the sun. It could be seen from miles away.

An illustration shows one possible way the pyramids may have been built.

Historians have other ideas, too. Some think the Egyptians built ramps on the insides of the pyramids. Some think the Egyptians used **water power**. Others think they used **hoists**. But no one can prove these ideas. Historians continue to search for the truth.

# CHAPTER 3

# A HUGE PROJECT

Building the Giza Pyramids required thousands of people. Many of them were highly skilled. They worked on the pyramids year-round. Other workers were unskilled. Each year, the Nile River flooded Egypt's farmland. This left farmers out of work for two months. So, they worked on the pyramids instead.

**The pharaoh may have watched while workers built the pyramids.**

Workers lived in a nearby temporary city. The city had houses, bakeries, and other buildings. Workers were paid and fed. They ate beef, sheep, and goats. They also ate large amounts of bread. Workers even had access to doctors and dentists.

Cities across Egypt may have helped with the project. They likely sent workers, food, and other resources. They did this to honor the pharaohs. Ancient Egyptians believed pharaohs became gods after they died. The pyramids were meant to help the pharaohs enter the next life. Treasure was meant to help, too. The pharaohs had their tombs filled with silver and gold.

Workers may have used ships to transport the pyramids' huge stone blocks.

When a pharaoh died, his body was prepared. This process was called mummification. Priests removed moisture from the body. Then they wrapped the body in strips of cloth. Lastly, the body was placed in a stone coffin. Mummification helped prevent **decay**.

Most Egyptians at this time were not mummified. The process was used only for members of the royal family. These people were buried in tombs near the pyramids. Workers were buried in tombs in the workers' city.

## GIZA ABANDONED

The Middle Kingdom lasted from approximately 2000 to 1650 BCE. During this period, Giza was abandoned. People broke into the tombs and pyramids. They stole the treasure. Pharaohs of the Middle Kingdom tore down parts of each complex. They used the stone for their own projects. In the New Kingdom (approximately 1550–1075 BCE), these actions were prohibited. The new pharaohs wanted to **preserve** the pyramids.

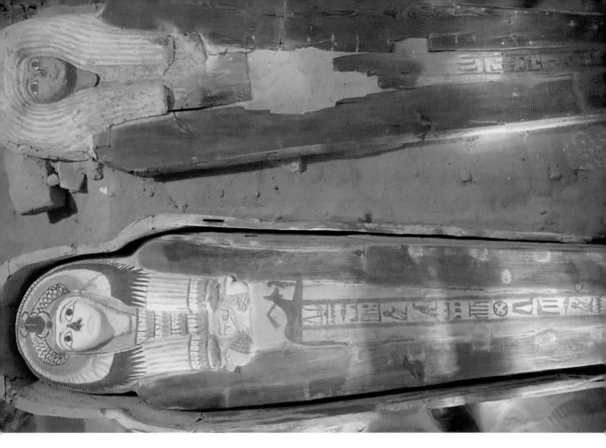

Archaeologists uncovered the tombs of important officials in a cemetery near the pyramids.

Each of the Giza Pyramids took 15 to 20 years to build. They required huge amounts of resources. But after King Menkaure, not enough resources were left. The next pharaoh was buried in a smaller, simpler tomb.

# EXCAVATING GIZA

Archaeologists learn about history from old items, or artifacts. They look for artifacts in the ground. Digging for artifacts is called excavation. The Giza Pyramids have been excavated many times. Some excavations were done by **colonists**. They sometimes stole the artifacts they found. Older excavations also damaged the pyramids. Today, excavations focus on preservation. Archaeologists use robots to explore the pyramids.

Archaeologists at Giza have learned much about ancient Egypt. They found ancient tools, pottery, and animal bones. These items give clues about how ancient Egyptians lived. Archaeologists also learn from tomb art. The tombs near the pyramids often had symbols carved into them. They showed images of farming, fishing, and religious practices.

Archaeologists excavate an ancient tomb in Giza.

In 2020, a museum in Scotland found an
artifact from Giza. It was a 5-inch (13-cm) piece of
wood. Colonists took this artifact from the Great
Pyramid in the 1800s. Archaeologists believe it is
more than 5,000 years old.

# CHAPTER 4

# THE PYRAMIDS TODAY

The Giza Pyramids have survived many challenges. Over time, the materials have aged. Rain and wind across the centuries have caused the stones to **degrade**. Earthquakes have also shaken the area. They weakened the pyramids. Some stones cracked in half. Other stones fell off entirely.

The Great Sphinx and the Giza Pyramids are slowly wearing away due to erosion.

Damage has also been caused by humans. Many people have moved to the cities around Giza. As the cities grew, water pipes were added underground. When pipes leak, groundwater rises. Water erodes the land under the pyramids. Eventually, the pyramids could collapse.

## THE SHIP OF KHUFU

The Giza Pyramids each had a boat pit. Ancient Egyptians believed the pharaohs used the boats to travel to the next life. In 1954, an archaeologist discovered Khufu's ship. It was buried next to the Great Pyramid. In 2021, officials moved the ship to the Grand Egyptian Museum. Here, the ship could be better preserved.

Machines inside the pyramids help remove water droplets from visitors' breath.

Tourism affects the pyramids as well. Approximately two million tourists visit the pyramids each year. As tourists breathe, tiny water droplets leave their mouths. This water enters the air. It draws salt from the limestone. This process weakens the stones.

Even tourists' footsteps make an impact. Over time, footsteps cause walkways to break down. In the past, tourists could ride camels near the site. This, too, caused damage. Tourists also cause damage by breaking rules. Some tourists have tried to climb the pyramids. Some have dropped litter. Others have spray-painted the walls.

Tourism has benefits, too. When tourists visit, they learn about Egyptian history. They also help Egypt's **economy**. They spend money at local businesses. They buy tickets to see the pyramids. Some of the money is used to preserve these wonders.

Sometimes, the pyramids are closed to tourists. During this time, officials use

Tourists are not allowed to climb the pyramids, but some people still do.

vacuums to suck water from the air. Other times, the pyramids need repairs. But officials must be careful. Using the wrong materials can cause further damage. Lastly, tourists can help by following rules. Taking care of the pyramids will allow people to enjoy them for years to come.

# FOCUS ON
# THE GIZA PYRAMIDS

*Write your answers on a separate piece of paper.*

**1.** Write a sentence that describes the main ideas from Chapter 1.

**2.** How do you think the pyramids were built? Why?

**3.** Which of the following cannot be found in the Great Pyramid?

> **A.** the King's Chamber
> **B.** the Sphinx
> **C.** the Grand Gallery

**4.** What would happen if a body was not mummified?

> **A.** It would decay faster.
> **B.** It would decay slower.
> **C.** Nothing would happen.

*Answer key on page 32.*

# GLOSSARY

**chambers**
Small, private rooms used for a certain purpose.

**colonists**
People who move into an area and take control.

**complex**
A group of buildings on the same site.

**decay**
The process of rotting or breaking down.

**degrade**
To break down or lose strength.

**economy**
The system of goods, services, money, and jobs in a certain place.

**hoists**
Systems of ropes and pulleys used to lift things.

**pharaohs**
Rulers in ancient Egypt.

**preserve**
To protect something so that it does not change.

**water power**
Power that is produced by the weight and motion of water.

# TO LEARN MORE

## BOOKS

Gagne, Tammy. *Egyptian Gods, Heroes, and Mythology.* Minneapolis: Abdo Publishing, 2019.

Golkar, Golriz. *Your Passport to Egypt.* North Mankato, MN: Capstone Press, 2022.

Nardo, Don. *Ancient Egypt.* Lake Elmo, MN: Focus Readers, 2020.

## NOTE TO EDUCATORS

Visit **www.focusreaders.com** to find lesson plans, activities, links, and other resources related to this title.

# INDEX

**Answer Key: 1.** Answers will vary; **2.** Answers will vary; **3.** B; **4.** A